i wait for the river

i wait
for the
river

poems
Maryann Russo

Inspiration Pointe Press

Published by Inspiration Pointe Press,
an imprint of
Over and Above Creative Group, Los Angeles, CA
www.overandabovecreative.com

Copyright © 2016 by Maryann Russo. All rights reserved.
ISBN: 978-0-9968406-6-8
Library of Congress Control Number: 2016930464

This book contains material protected under International and Federal Copyright Laws and Treaties. No part of this publication may be reproduced, distributed, or transmitted in any form or by any means, including photocopying, recording, or other electronic or mechanical methods, without the prior written permission of the author, except in the case of brief quotations embodied in critical reviews and certain other noncommercial uses permitted by copyright law.

For permission requests, please email the publisher at following address:
rickbenzel@overandabovecreative.com.

For information, contact Over And Above Press,
8180 Manitoba Street, Unit 151, Playa del Rey, CA 90293.

Creative Director: Susan Shankin & Associates

First edition.
Printed in the United States of America

Visit us at www.OverAndAboveCreative.com
www.Facebook.com/MaryannRussoAuthor

Praise for *I Wait for the River*

A river can be many things. It can be both a conduit and source. In her opening poem, "The River," Maryann describes the wait as an ache, a desire tinged with fear. And so begins the journey. Maryann navigates a river that takes hostages, and is unrelenting as it winds through narrow channels. Yet just when it seems the river is too swift, the danger too real, she reminds us: "Don't dismiss the shadows cast across the shore." *Everything Passes. Dive.* You will be glad that you did.

SUSAN B. GILBERT, author of *Blue White Veil*

I Wait For The River is a collection embedded with the quiet passion of Zen. Its greatest strength lies in its ability to precisely and succinctly capture the turning points in life. The intersections between instances when possibilities are perceived and pivot points when choices are made come alive under Maryann's pen. It is ultimately about how to meet the tumbling uncertainties of a life-carrying river with a sense of purpose, acceptance, and awe: an approach that advocates discovery and embraces change. Crystalline in its beautiful descriptions, it is a roadmap to greeting the morning, surviving the darkness, and relishing all facets of life. Poetry enthusiasts with a background in meditation, Zen, and concepts of gratitude and acknowledgment will especially relish these pieces for their precision, seasonal connections, and, most of all, for their lovely illustrations of a blossoming life.

DIANE DONOVAN, Senior Reviewer, Midwest Book Review

Each poem in *I Wait for the River* is a little dose of medicine for the soul. Maryann's words calm the mind and soothe the spirit. Her writing takes us on a journey through both the whimsical lightness and heavy truths of human existence. These are poems to be read again and again.

MEREDITH KLEIN, Mindfulness Teacher, Life Coach

The beautiful abstract quality of Maryann's work has been a source of inspiration since I discovered her. She expresses with the stroke of a pen all the complex emotions I endeavor to express with the stroke of a brush. *I Wait For the River* will touch painters and poets and all those who love the natural world.

BARBARA CARDWELL, English Contemporary Abstract Painter

Maryann is a truly gifted poet. This collection resonates through one's being, awakening and enriching us. Her work is marvelously rhythmic, profoundly engaged, and powerfully disciplined. She masters the art of personal themes with sensitivity, deep spirituality, and an innate awareness of the human condition. Here is an artist to watch.

HARVEY JASON, Mystery Pier Books, Inc.

contents

Acknowledgments	xi
The River	1
My Heart	2
Heart of My Heart	3
In The Night	4
The Vulnerability of Morning	5
In the Stream	6
For Anne	7
Collision	9
Beyond	10
Counting	11
Practice	12
The Ground	13
Beyond Thoughts	14
Knowing	15
Snail	16
The Bee	17
The Search to Soothe	18

Spiral	*19*
Persevere	*20*
Flash	*21*
The Map	*22*
Ephemeral	*23*
The Gold	*24*
The Golden Hour	*25*
Kauai	*26*
Lahaina	*27*
Infinity	*28*
Shadows	*29*
Seamless	*30*
Retreat	*31*
Silent Celebrations	*32*
Lilies	*33*
Inside the Nest	*34*
Flight	*35*
Push and Pull	*36*
Light	*37*
Song	*38*
The Roof	*39*
Joe Redota Trail	*40*
Everything Passes	*41*
Show Up	*42*
After the Exhale	*43*

Gratitude	*44*
Sweet Sister	*45*
For Susan	*46*
Growing Love	*47*
Genesis	*48*
If	*49*
Questions	*50*
Sway Me	*51*
Instructions	*52*
Corme Royal—Mid-September	*53*
Frame	*54*
This Day	*55*
Fall	*56*
Anew	*57*
Birthday of My Mother	*58*
Clouds	*59*
Cambria Cypress	*60*
Wings (for Olivia)	*61*
Barbara	*62*
Ocean	*63*
One	*64*
Dive	*65*
Meditation	*66*
Afterword	*67*
About the Author	*69*

acknowledgments

With gratitude to the editors of the following publications, where some of my work first appeared:

Soul-Lit — "Collision"

River Poets Journal — "Dance" from Maryann's first book *Wild and Still* has been chosen for the special edition of *Signature Poems*

Pace — "My Heart"

Poetic Diversity — "Wings," "Light" and "Spiral"

Blue Lyra Review — "Joe Redota Trail"

cardwellartfrance.com, the website for contemporary artist Barbara Cardwell — "Barbara"

Origami Poems Project 2016 contest — "The River"
The Best of Kindness Anthology

NAMI Newsletter — "For Anne" and "The Ground"

Amygdala Literary Magazine — "Beyond Thoughts" and "The Golden Hour"

Thank you Deborah Edler Brown, midwife and
guide for my poems before they meet the world.

Thank you to my readers,
Olivia La Bouff,
Linda Saker,
Laura Roe Stevens,
Cheryl Tcir, and
Samatha Lamberg
for your careful reading and insights.

Thank you to Julie Russo for your technological
and enthusiastic support.

Thank you to my many mentors and
inspirations and unconditional encouragers.

Thank you to my family, whose love keeps me going:
brothers Ron and John;
sister Theresa,
daughter Anne, and
husband Mike.

The River

I wait for the river
to wash over me
to carry me
through its descending rapids

but I am afraid

of the rocks
jutting out of its folds
and the sharp edges
of fallen branches

My feet feel
the grit of the shallows
and I wonder
what else lies there
to cut or to sting

I want the river
to carry me with kindness
around the bends
and trees that bow
from the banks

carry me safely
all the way
to the sea

My Heart

enlarged and scarred
is what the mapping showed

my heart
beating wild
and uncertain

wanting to stay
the rhythm it was
neat and balanced

until it wasn't

the stripping away of certainty
showed the size
and scarring
I did not want to expose

in the stripping away
glistens
the truth

bare, fragile,
human

Heart of My Heart

Vessels,
chambers hold
the rhythm of my days
hidden
pulsing
asking the same question:

Will you let your breath
and these measured beatings
accelerating
slowing

these echoes
of what you could not cry?

will you allow
this heart
to open you?

In The Night

I am held hostage
by stillness and
an idle body

Thoughts rattle
about like birds that have
outgrown their nests

Sleep hovers
over the onslaught of mind
hoping to settle

The Vulnerability of Morning

Have you ever felt
the vulnerability of early morning
the sun fresh and rising
after bringing its lamp to
the other side of the sea?

Dew illumines
grass and leaves
If my breath allows
my spirit also rises

not yet troubled
by the download of worries
that line up,
racehorses at the gate

There is a slit
through which a peek
of sky
can wrap its heart
around me

beyond thoughts
beyond words

in the exaltation of silence

In the Stream

Time moves on like the stream,
unrelenting, through stones.
If they stay in the river's bed
the rocks become smooth.
Here I am in another day
listening for gulls
and the erratic whir of
hummingbird wings,
immersing myself
in these currents
with kindness
as my staff.

For Anne

The waves pound relentlessly
one after the other
their origins from
who knows where

The hidden recesses of the waters
arch, gather, crash, expel
dissolve, recede, erupt

Words she has used
to describe the folly
of her mind

This madness that brews
and spits and rolls
must have its way
as the mania mounts
and the medicine
tries to temper

She holds tight
a tiny raft
in the tempest storms
of her head

She fears she will go under
tossed by the last slam
She wants to go under
deep, below the fury
and menacing highs

There is hope–
she knows that calm
awaits like a blanket
that she is not alone

that somehow the waves
belong to a sea beyond
where her mind
takes her

Collision

The mind collides
again
with the heart
    tender
    expansive

the mind blazes its way
with all it thinks it knows

a lanky tractor
edging the lush green
to a buzz cut

While the heart
    run over
    again
waits
for any opening
    a pause
    one long exhale
    reverse gear

to invite the mind
    to hear
    listen

then follow

Beyond

I wish to surrender
to the expanse
of all I do not know

But I fear
clouds can't hold me
stars will singe me
fish swallow me
or pure emptiness
lose me

So I teeter
on the speck
of what
I think I know

the tiny perceptions
my dark pupils allow

mere wisps
which can never
carry me

Counting

My father sat in his chair
in the left corner of the living room,
head tilted skyward,
twirling his forefinger.

One day he announced
        he was counting
        the holes in the ceiling

I too count
        miles walked
        potato chips on a plate
        pounds on the scale
        minutes late
        bees in the garden
        days until my birthday

Why would we count
 unless we wanted some number

that might tell us something
we need to know?

Practice

The months melt into each other
and the ache of time
throbs on.

In youth I wished
to nudge time along
hurry it through adolescence
to the numbers that seemed
to carry privilege and passage.

Now I long for the ease
of childhood
plump with possibility

to chase a bird across the sand
until it lifts in relief
to squat in a field
investigate life in miniature
ants trolling in formation
wildflowers waiting to be plucked.

I want to practice what I knew then
to be in the only moment I can be
with these words
and the rich bounty of space
between words
where the wildflower still waits.

The Ground

You want to live
on the ground you know
the path clearly worn
the sights familiar
and the sea
deep, blue
at a distance.

Then grief comes,
a thief in broad daylight

and the ground
becomes one
you do not know
but must walk.

There is nothing predictable
about this earth
crumbling beneath your step
and the sea
now closer,
waves arching.

You look for a way
to turn back
to find what you lost.

You must greet
this ground.

Beyond Thoughts

Beyond thoughts
and the timepieces
that command my
comings and goings

the mountains
sit in their jagged stillness
as if they simply
arrived that way

The sky is a
vast blue
swaddling us all

I veer away
from this thought–
we are but
a speck of dirt

whirling
unseen
in the galaxies

uncertain
of where we are going

Knowing

The leaves
in their vulnerability
wait for the water
that will raise them.

Can we be as patient
knowing we need more
than water
to soak our roots?

Snail

The glare of the sun
beats upon the tiny shell
as it pushes across
the wet universe of lawn
amongst the vast grass blades

to risk its soft body
inside the illusion of its casing
to reach the unknown earth
of the garden which calls
from across the cement path

The Bee

My body rises and falls
to receive the breath
so fleeting.
As does the breast
of the bird which propels
its wings in the same air,
and the tiny bee
with only seven weeks
to make a drop of honey.

The Search to Soothe

I landed hard in this world
through channels
narrow and anxious

Mother said I was
the most difficult delivery
my brand new body
pushing toward the light

Now I give birth to words
still moving
away from constriction

into soft skies
simple glides
a need to view
vast seas

to linger in silence
and the compassion
that calls me
back to center

Spiral

I am drawn
to the deep down design
of the nautilus

a tight circle
revolving around itself
seeming to arrive and start
from the same place

a labyrinth
which takes us always
to the center
past a place
we have been before

my spiral courses
within

an unknown path
taking me beyond
blood and bones

into the core

Persevere

I must persevere
the way waves do
carried by their currents
rolling as they come
crashing or crawling
to blend with the shore

the way peonies
hold themselves
in tight bulbs
then unpetal quickly

Even in their weathered fullness
they are beautiful
expecting nothing
exposing their secrets to the sun

Flash

The rapid movement of her wings
punctuates the flower

The flower will know
the butterfly was deeply
present

That's all the butterfly
can do
in her short span here

a flutter and swoon,
a flash of wings

The Map

Where was the map
she wondered,
paths clearly marked?

You are the map
she heard.
The lines and creases
emerging on her face

evidence of the erosions
of smiles and frowns,
gravity
which if nothing else
kept her grounded

in the landscape where she stood
knowing
she already contained
all she needed for the journey.

Silence would reveal
the compass
her heart become the guide.

She came to see
why the butterfly
is so elusive.

Ephemeral

The leaves shimmy
on their branches
Clouds descend
to blot the orange-pink
sunset.

We sit and sip
as if this would
always be the case

here

all grace
and golden

The Gold

We are here
to grow toward
our own disappearance

slipping out
like the friend
who left
while having gelato in Aruba

There will be the day
when you are no longer here
awake to the whisper of leaves
after the wind has passed

alert to the way an old cypress
bends to the ground
as if to bow to
your presence

So taste the warm bread
and soft butter
the first bite
of dark chocolate

linger with the sun as it dips
with a hug wrapped around you

look through everything
to find the gold

The Golden Hour

The shades are drawn
to deflect the sun
as it drifts down
in the late afternoon

Darkness is bound to come
to douse the light

Photographers
find in shadow
and this last brightness
a place of clarity

Just before
the inevitable dusk

Kauai

Palm fronds bend
and flutter
while clouds
float above the sea

Ribbons of waves
curl towards the shore
white noise of ocean
lulls the illusion

as if something were not
always changing
as if anything
could stay the same

Lahaina

A half moon
hangs
in the clear dark sky
her features chiseled
Forlorn eyes
face into the universe
with a slight smile
surrounded
by a pool of her
own light

Infinity

How wide the reach
with nothing to grasp

though words
try to wrap around

though words
are flung

to catch
even one star

Shadows

Don't dismiss the shadows
cast across the shore

or behind the flames
all fuss and fire

dark silent replicas
can mesmerize

dance with you
accompany you like a friend

tell you
not to fear the darkness

Seamless

The waves are seamless
as they complete their last laps
onto the shore
one follows the other
before dissipating

I want to believe that life
is seamless
despite ruptures
of the heart
the random rise and fall
of its waves

that it is always
one with the sea

Retreat

I search the tops of trees
for swaying leaves
look for the day moon
faint and white
and watch for any bird that lands
heavy on a thin branch
slightly tipping it
I keep my head up
where it is vast
and timeless

Silent Celebrations

The tree extols
each season
from the unseen seedling
to solid trunk
spindly branches

it flowers and thickens
with age
bares itself in autumn
with necessary shedding

it withstands winter
in sheer anticipation
that green
will come again

through the energy
of its own center
in the sitting
in the waiting

Lilies

The lilies lean into the light,
extending the ears of their centers

as if listening to secrets
only they can hear.

Inside the Nest

A perfect precarious nest sits
on a slight branch of the rose bush,
on leaves speckled with aphid bites.
Mother hummingbird perches,
her head alert,
her needle beak tilting upward,
then flits away in a millisecond.
Inside the miniature cubby
there is tiny furry movement.
Baby hearts beating,
waiting for wings.

Flight

The hummingbirds fled.

Over weeks their mother
had roosted on two tiny eggs.

One day all that remained
was a dribble of shell.
The babies grew quickly
sprouting fur on their bare flesh.

They cuddled
awaiting feeding time
beaks poised skyward
as if in silent song.

I did not see
their departure
the first dance of their wings
only the mosaic
of an empty nest.

Push and Pull

Gravity pulls us to earth;
so does light draw our sight
as it spills from the sun
before setting.

A purple hibiscus pulls
our gaze into its
deep yellow center.

A mother eagle pushes
her baby from the nest
into the wide air
        without invitation
        without warning

How does the eaglet know
to lift its tiny wings
enough to fly?

Light

Everything reaches
to the light that calls it,
the invisible moon at night
or any sliver that spills through
the blinds

Wings lift to tree tops and
roof peaks
Leaves rise in their slow stretch
toward the sun
Petals of certain flowers
open only with morning

Everything reaches
to the light that calls it
As we move
into each day
even with bleakness
discomfort or doubt

there is some glimmer
from within

Song

you loiter
on the bare branch
looking for a sign of green
and the voice
you once had

tight-winged
afraid the song
has gone

sing little bird

a melody will come
from the place
you do not know

the bleak morning
is studded with
music

and waits
for you

The Roof

The wind rips off the roof
and darkness pervades

A siege of moonless nights
Fair game for the rain

Does one hope
that a new roof will cover,

For the first piece of moon
to cast light,

Or to see whatever
the sky brings?

Joe Redota Trail

A pair of wings
flutters flashes
of gold and orange

Brown leaves
cling to their trees
even as green
overtakes them

A rusted chain
hangs from an old
wooden post

White wild daisies
pop from the
edges of concrete

One blue jay
takes its chances
and hops across the road

My heart wants
to close

It opens
to whatever season
comes

Everything Passes

the sad and the mad
the glimpses of glad
move through you
visit again
in some other disguise

run all you want
at some point
you will need to sit on a rock
and catch your breath

you will discard
your garments
because of their
rip and tear

you will become
a river
feel the flow
of all that you are

Show Up

Show up just this way
with your runaway mind
and floundering humanity

You do not know
where the train is going
and what you thought
would be
is miles away from
what is

Show up

The gray roots
of your ruffled hair
exposed

Unable to sit still
when the perfect meditation
calls for
no mind

And your self
wanders the dark day
with a longing
that has no name
loose threads
without a tapestry

Show up just this way
The way that you are
is the way in

After the Exhale

the slip and slide
of air
the last relinquishment
of oxygen

there is a second
of stillness
deflation
a moment filled
only with
trust

that the next breath
awaits

to feed you
to open again
your heart
which wants to
unfold

Gratitude

I am grateful for all that is within
and without
for the awareness of space
beyond the appearance of things,
space to dissolve and evolve,
to disappear and emerge

undefined by this body
which I bump around in
mistreat, rearrange,
and deny its eventual decline.

I am grateful for this body
that has been lent to me
carrying the blood and bones
of my descent.

I am grateful for my soul,
unseen, indefinable,
ascending Self,
silent Everything.

I promise to listen more deeply
to its inaudible whisperings.

I am most grateful
for the ever-longing,
which has brought this
exhilaration of souls
who accompany me.

Sweet Sister

Your limbs
cast shadows
dark and thin

Your eyes wide
and endless
take me to your soul

Through the shallows
and neck high rivers
you have survived

I wish for you
my sight
which sees you
like the roses
that line your garden

wild and fragrant
branches bending
across the path

For Susan

Fennel and kale
fresh salmon from the farmer's market
and seeds planted
to sprout parsley and rosemary
words strung together
to make poetry of your world

Henry Miller and cancer
lost loves, marigolds
all seeds to grow
what you would find
in the rich dark earth
of your heart

bared slightly
and spilling over

Growing Love

Do I grow love,
planted with water and sun,
rich soil and time,
as love sprouts
then opens?

Or does love grow me
through travails of years
and searching?

When I was not paying attention,
love had my back
shattered my heart
and the shards
became a rainbow prism
shining and
recognizing itself
wherever love went

which I discovered
was everywhere
as the seed
in the dark earth
held the flower
all along.

Genesis

You cannot get by
without the fire

The fire will lure you
into its blazing center
where you thought
you did not want to go
where you feel the scorch
of what you held dearest
go to cinders

That is the paradox
of ashes

One word rises
from the heap
      live
and another
      love

You finally know
nothing else is needed

they become
your beginning

If

If we have wings
to lift us out of the
stark perceptions
the ground and gravity
that hold us

If we have wings
to lighten the dark
that pins us
to the mat

If we have wings
they come not
from our arms
which the wind
will not carry

If we truly have wings
they are the sisters
who listen
who let us ride
the open hearts
of their compassion

who bring us
to the sky

Questions

Can you allow yourself
to be hijacked by love
every sense ignited,
then left in a ditch
smoldering?

Can you allow yourself
to be swindled by the wind,
whipped from the safe road
to the one direction
you do not want to go?

Can you consent
to be tossed by the currents
fearing the chaos
and tumble of waves

to be taken
where the river
wants to carry you?

Sway Me

Sway me the way
a Hawaiian breeze bends
palm fronds to and fro
like unsettled hair.

Sway me the way
a lover seduces,
arms around the waist,
drawing closer
to a heart beating fast,

The way I imagine
my Irish mother swayed my Italian father
when she first made spaghetti
and meatballs from scratch,
the aroma, an elixir
that would keep him.

Sweet and inviting,
smooth and flexible,
the difference between a singing brook
and the dam breaking.

Instructions

Fall into anything
as if you were just walking along
minding your own business
and a pebble or a boulder
tripped you out of your lull

and you fall

this is the path to love
to what is true in you

the jolt takes you
out of the slow dribble
and into the full stream

that carries you to the place
you were resisting
carries you from the mindless trance
you call living

fall
wake up
open your eyes
finally see

Corme Royal—Mid-September

Fields brim with sunflowers
once flared with gold
they now bow their heads
loyal to the sun

ready to let go
of their seeds
and another season

Across the narrow path
vineyards are heavy
with green
and grapes
soon to surrender
to their harvest

and to the hands that will pick them
that will grasp the stems of glasses
filled with their wine
hold the brushes
that will paint them
into still life

Frame

I like the frame that my windowpane makes,
the scene changing each moment
as I look through the shutters.
An oleander tree bursts with white buds in midsummer
and softens the fence and garages behind them.
If there is a breeze,
it livens the still life
brings sway to the leaves.

Passersby stroll
on the path between streets.
Sometimes they peer in–
I peek out–
we pretend not to see each other.
Even on a down day
I can acknowledge the sun,
see whatever presents itself,
this sauce of humanity,
the old window screen
torn and askew.

This Day

I watch my mind
lean into the morning

as if the summer foliage
would always be here
crawling green everywhere

and I
queen of my day
smooth the ecru sheets

stride with my breath
into the living room

its walls and windows
the only things
separating me

from the world
which awaits

Fall

Fall into the deep center
of the Georgia O'Keefe flower
butter yellow

into the glossy folds
of the waves
that promise to carry you

the warm grainy sands
which will not swallow you
but remind you the earth is your ground

Fall into your own exhalation
this breath sustains you
as long as you are here

Anew

As the heater whirrs
to warm the house
and I sip hot java
from a large ceramic mug
a friend lies in her hospital bed
sleeping a timeless sleep

This day stretches before me
alive with breath
and plans

I step into these hours
seeing anew

> the way each scarlet grape
> is round and cold
> before it releases its sweetness

> the way more light is cast
> into my living room
> after the ficus is trimmed bare

> the way the ocean offers
> itself in its wide expanse
> willing to hold everything

Birthday of My Mother

We no longer
have to try

You on the other side
relieved
forgiven

Me here

releasing this heritage
of trying
        to be good
        to be seen
        to be more

Do the waves
try to move with the wind

or these birds
with their red tufts
to sing sweet songs?

Clouds

Swarms of clouds
congregate

form hearts and dragons
dissipate

I come to know
what I already know

release
the strangle of thoughts

let them become clouds
join the sky

Cambria Cypress

The cypress
do not worry
if they are special.

They bow
with the windswept years
to listen
closer to the ground.

Wings
(for Olivia)

Seventy has wings
wide and etched
with all the ages
you have ever been

Pinions carved
by angst and joy
chinks in what
you thought was armor
give lift for flight

into skies
expansive enough to hold
the questions that remain
endless and open
which you cannot carry
because they would
slip through your grasp

Leaving this moment
to love

you find that
nothing can be filled

only emptied
again
and again

Barbara

she paints in her attic studio
at the top of a coil
of narrow stairs

creates palettes of turquoise
and magenta
a smear of yellow
streaks across her canvas
a bird, she says

whatever is within
spreads across her work
without permission
wide and awake
like her eyes

if I had to name it
I would call it
joy

Ocean

I wait for the deepening tide
to pull its waters
further into the sea
leaving the glistening shore
punctuated with trails of seaweed
and the flies that rest there

they lift in a flurry
when I run by
then settle again

the low tides
allow my entry
invite me to venture
into the mystery
of what keeps the ocean
in its place

no one knows
the depths
it holds

only that its surface
reflects the sky

One

There is no way
to meet anything
except with love

the way the sky
meets the ocean
as if they were one

Dive

There is nothing left to do
but dive.
Do not tarry
or dip a toe into the water.
Dive into the whimsy
that only wants
to carry you
if you will relax
into its wet folds.

Stones have been carved
by the rush of water over time.
They did nothing
but lie in the river's bed,
allowing their edges
to become smooth.

Become one
with the river
the dancing, downstream
singing waters
clear, soothing, relentless
soon to empty
into the sea.

Meditation

The mind
is a million fish
forging upstream
spilling downstream
again
and again

while the river
carries them all

afterword

The river waits
to take me through
its tumble-down waters

uncertain of obstacles
uncertain of when
I will spill out to the sea

about the author

Maryann Russo's poems have appeared in numerous publications. One of her poems was nominated for the prestigious Pushcart Prize. Her first collection of poems, *Wild And Still*, was published in 2013. She is a psychotherapist who lives in Palos Verdes Estates, CA.

Visit Maryann at www.Facebook.com/MaryannRussoAuthor

If you enjoyed reading this book,
we appreciate your review of it on Amazon
and on other book review websites.

www.ingramcontent.com/pod-product-compliance
Lightning Source LLC
Chambersburg PA
CBHW071740040426
42446CB00012B/2416